Debt Busters

Effective Tips To Help You Finally Get Out From Under The Clutches Of Debt!

Table Of Contents

Introduction

Have you managed to slip into big bad debt? There's no denying that debt put you in a state of unrest and anxiety. Burying your head into the sand is not enough to ridden the burdening loans. You must bounce back with a plan to recoup your debts one at a time. It isn't as hard-won as you imagine. A little planning and practical tricks can pull you out of the abyss in no time.

Wondering how to crawl out of the debt situation? Scrolling through the tips listed below could be a good start. However, before you mindlessly put these tips into practice, there's some serious thinking to do.

You must snip all ties with debts right away. No more credit cards, personal loans, or mindless shopping. Breaking up with debts is a cakewalk. Stop spending riches on materials you don't really need. Switch your spending habits and fix your mistakes for starters.

Hit the pause to your borrowing habits

Stop borrowing money. Little do you realize that you are drowning in deep debts. Not sure how you are asking for extra funds? Well, the thrill of swiping your credit cards sums up your borrowing attitude. Taking out loans to shop or sail through a pleasurable life? Stop and think - are loans or added credits any different from borrowing?

Figure and change your attitude towards money. Realize that bringing home the bacon is way more essential than shopping for exquisite designer merchandise. Try and sustain on cash. It works wonders in dwindling your spending habits. Living on cash is far better than being cash-strapped, don't you agree? One cool way to kick-start controlling your debts is to chop up the credit cards and toss them out.

How To Not Be In Debt Right Now?

A not-so-impressive financial standing is a struggle to deal with. But, big debts can wreck your peace of mind. Don't you agree? Slipping into bad debt is not always due to losing control of your money. Sudden unwelcome circumstances like a medical crisis or a layoff in a job are financially burdening too. Regardless, carrying the load of a big fat debt is mentally draining. Do you feel crippled or bankrupt? Reckon there is no way to crawl out of the problem? Stop and breathe! A little planning and diligence can work wonders in freeing you from the monetary stress.

How to clear the credits and be financially stable yet again?

1. Strategize ways to dodge the crisis

Debts amplify when you are not regular in settling the dues. The interests shoot up in a blink of an eye. Sit back and prepare a list of the debts you owe. Do not miss counting the trivial dues too. It can add up and cost you riches in the long run. Categorize the debts that must be squared off urgently. Is there a loan that's burning holes in the wallets by charging you a swanky interest? Might as well pay off the loan first. Settling smaller debts that are not-so-burdening is a good idea too. It cuts the list short.

Wondering how will you wiggle a tight budget and pay off the dues? Knowing the ins and outs of budgeting play a big role. Track your expenses, come up with a financial plan that's realistic and easy to follow. Stay clear from the pitfalls when setting a budget. If you are not quite handy at chalking out a budget, use the assistance of professional consultants.

2. Stop being a waster and earn the big bucks

Are you forking out more money than you should? Probably a good reason that's made you strapped and indebted in the first place. Being mindful of how much you spend matters big. Are your earnings not enough to support your expenses? Now is the time to take up extra gigs and start bagging in more money.

Cutting down a few minor insignificant things can save you good cash. For instance, little do you realize frittering out riches on takeaways. Why don't you plan your meals at home using fresh groceries? Does it irk you to think of ways to square off multiple loans? Choose to consolidate your dues into one.

3. Clear your debts in the right way

Are you of the idea that slush funds to someone important can dwindle your dues? Incorrect! Debts must be settled out of your pockets. To make the process slightly less hard-won, list your debts as per the priorities. A credit card charging you riches as interests? Square off the dues on your credit card first and toss out the card. Handling one debt at a time is less taxing and hassle-free. Settling the shorter debts first is already a half-battle won. Keep tabs on your progress and set small milestones to be accomplished before hitting the easy street.

Silly Things You Didn't Realize You Spent A Fortune On

Little did you realize that misspending on the dumbest thing has cost you riches in the past. Unfortunately, the mistakes are still on a roll and so are the expenses. Wondering which brainless expenses are being talked about? Let's take a quick look:

1. Weekend movie treats

Stepping out for a movie and a pleasure-filled moment with family is a swanky expense. Confused? Scoring tickets for four is the first big expense. The coke and popcorn to snack upon cost you big bucks. Choose a recliner and the cost spirals. In short, a one-time movie with the fam is a pricey affair.

2. Magazines and books

Did you know that the local library up the streets is home to myriads of books and magazines? Paying extra for the books or the magazines stacked in the library hardly makes sense. It's up for grabs or can be rented at dirt cheap prices.

3. The outrageously priced gym membership

Are you struggling to trim the flabs? Doing the hard drills in a gym is not a pressing need. Strenuous rounds of jog or a walk in the park work wonders in scaling down the pounds. Opting for an expensive gym membership and not likely using it is no less than burning your money. Unfortunately, memberships like such are recurring and keep rolling unless you cancel the membership.

4. Multiple subscription services add up

Do you have a bunch of subscription services? Paying out riches for recreation hardly makes sense. How often do you subscribe to a plan, use it a couple of times, and forget about it? Juggling between several subscription services is difficult. The payments are mostly on autopay. Result? Your expenses continue to add up although the services are not utilized. Too lazy to unsubscribe? You certainly know how to sink your money mindlessly and embrace debt.

5. Surplus bank fee

Transaction charges are one thing. However, isn't it dumb to pay a bank to keep your hard-earned money? Bearing the brunt of an expensive service fees is uncalled for. Start hunting for a different bank instead. Numerous credit unions are in business offering zero-fee banking services. The banking fee that appears trivial now is enough to burn a hole in your account.

6. Impulsive in-app purchases

How often are you engrossed playing games on phone? Do you buy equipment to get ahead in the game or purchase apps in the spur of the moment? The teeny-tiny app charges add up to an overwhelming cost. Blowing up your earnings for useless app purchases paves the way for debts to creep in.

7. The cable costs

When Netflix and chill is in vogue all across the globe, why on earth are you still stuck to your TV cable? Shelling out $50 a month is no inexpensive affair. Does it sound worth the money to watch a show or two at times? A hard no! Look for cheaper alternatives and ditch your cable.

8. Takeaways and junk

It is no secret that a homemade burger is not as scrumptious as a fast-food eatery one. But, it is no good for your health too. Sadly, you pay hefty amounts for junk food and sparing for the everyday grocery.

Stop making the dumb calls and put your money in the right place. Stay out of debts too.

Can A Balance Transfer Bail You Out From Surging Credit Card Bills?

Is balance transfer your parachute to safety for burning debts? The importance of balance transfer has been spelled out on numerous occasions. Little did you know that the credit card tool is promising and saves you from footing the hiked interests.

In short, balance transfer is a recommended strategy to dip your credit card dues quickly.

Do you know enough about balance transfer?

Before speaking volumes of balance transfer and its perks, are you familiar with the process? Signing over an outstanding debt on a loan or a credit card to a different card sums up the description of a balance transfer. It is mostly a new card that bills consumers with a significant cut-back in the interest rates.

Debtors struggle to square off multiple credit card bills. The swanky interests charged are killing for the consumers to settle. Default in repaying the balances earns you a degrading credit score. A balance transfer card simplifies the hassles of clearing multiple debts. It consolidates the outstanding charges on loans and credit cards into a single debt. Cherry on the cake - the lowly interest rates make it easy to pay off the outstanding balance.

Points to look into before you agree to resort to balance transfer

Balance transfer is mostly a win-win. But, learning of the downsides play a big role too. It is easy to be lured into purchasing a credit card that promises zero interest on balance transfer. Can you overlook the details though? If you have had a messy experience with a loan or a card previously, you could end up footing penalties and striking rates of interest. Is your name on the list of defaulters? Have you used up surplus credit? In a nutshell, defaulters are not always offered lucrative promotional interest rates.

Dig into the details before you say yes to balance transfer. Check if you are being charged with penalty payments or if there's a leg up in the rates of interest. Here are a few points to mull over before you jump into the option of a balance transfer.

1. Is there a hefty upfront fee?

Ordinarily, carrying a balance from one card to another levy a charge. It could be reasonable, swanky, or nil, depending on the company you choose to settle your debt scores with. A standard 3%-5% fee is okay. Stay on toes if the interests billed are costlier than the standard percentage.

Not too sure if agreeing to the promotional rates on a balance transfer is a good idea? You can save big in the long term and recoup the costs of transaction fees.

2. Will the promotional interest rates seize?

Companies assist debtors with promotional cutbacks in the interests levied on balance transfers. Unfortunately, the offer stands for a limited time only. The low-interest perks are mostly available for tenures like 9 months or more. Keep tabs on how long the dwindling rate of interest is up for grabs. Try and clear off a chunk of your debts within the promotional tenure. It scales up your savings by large.

3. Can problems strike you when the promotional interest rates discontinue?

Expiry of the discounted introductory interests is a bummer. Is it easy to square off the debts when interests spike from zero to 15% out of the blue? Certainly not! This is why reading the details of the agreement matters big before signing up for a balance transfer.

Mistakes To Avoid When Digging Out Of Debt

Have you decided to kiss goodbye to the piling dues? Congratulations! Winning financial freedom is not very distant. Tumbling into debts is not always in your hand. What matters is how adept are you in crawling out of the straining finances. Calling the right shots and making the right financial layout makes settling debts a cakewalk.

Unfortunately, repeating the rookie mistakes will keep sinking your money. Paying off the big fat dues can be overwhelming. Not hitting the pause button on your reckless habits will land you in bigger debts. Can you afford to shell out riches when you are cash-strapped? No! Putting an end to your mistakes helps you clear your debts in a spry.

Here's what you must avoid:

1. Your long habit of careless spending

Your reckless spending pattern has pushed you into a world of debts and problems? Now is the time to change course and be a strategic thinker instead. Don't fork out money without a thought. A little thinking keeps you from being the spendthrift that you are.

* Figure the difference between needs and desire

* Break-off from impulsive buys

* Save by prepping meals at home

Have you been a high roller all your life? Pretty much explains what puts your finances on the spot. Of course, the transformation from being a wastrel to being economical is not an overnight thing. But, start cutting down your spending now. Freeing up your money gives you extra cash to clear off the loans.

2. Trying to pay off too many dues in one shot

Are you desperate to pay off the debts at once? Stacking up multiple credit cards and taking out too many loans have already crippled your financial standing. Your plate is pretty full. Trying to pay off the dues will puzzle you. What's worse? The cash crunch is real and you will have no emergency funds to fall back.

Wondering how to tackle financial obligations like a pro?

- Start listing your debts. Small or hefty, all dues must be on the list
- Rank your debts as per the priorities. Loans charging you a hefty interest must be at the top of the list, followed by dues with less-swankier interests.
- Clear off the dues with the smallest balance first.

Settling the debts with the highest interest is recommended too. Once the debt is squared off, you free up a large chunk of money. Paying off all other dues is easy then.

3. Not having a budget to tackle debts

Figuring out an effective financial plan is the most significant tool when battling the odds of fat debts. Without a good budget, falling into the pit of debts and dues is only obvious.

Creating a financial plan is not as herculean as you picture. It's all about listing the deets. For instance, write down your earnings. List the bills that come like clockwork each month. Leave a small budget to pay for the unanticipated miscellaneous stuff. What's remaining are the funds that you must set aside for the rainy days. The objective is to earn more and dish out less money.

Don't worry about debt being a strangling life-long sentence. Pull yourself out of the richly money dues. Proper plans and diligence will help you sail through the crisis.

Is Budgeting Enough To Pull You Out Of Debt?

Is your current financial situation up for a toss? Wondering if planning the right budget can save you from drowning in debts? Well, it's certainly a start but planning alone is not enough to hit the mark. A well-thought strategy is a dire need. Budgeting is not as easy as it sounds. Turning blind to the money that rolls into and out of your account is difficult. Can you put a stop to your spending habits out of the blue? Hard! Fixing upon a number that could save you big bucks and clear your debts is not an erratic decision. Budgeting is all about strategizing your earnings and expenses. Nipping your careless spending habits in the bud is a pressing need. Planning your investments right plays a pivotal part too.

Unfortunately, the myths related to the budgeting do's and don'ts are quite a few. It influences your budget preps in a not-so-favorable way. Aren't you curious to learn about the misbeliefs?

Busting facts that are reckoned normal

1. Leeways are a big no in budgeting

It is a no-brainer that being strict with your money plan is key to put an end to your debts. You can no longer be a spendthrift and shell out fat money on a game that's new in the market. Curbing your expenses matters big when preparing a budget to sustain. However, can you kiss goodbye to all fun and merry things in life? You will undoubtedly go nuts and crazy. Leaving rooms to fit in small discretionary expenses is essential too.

Your primary budget is not carved in stone. Multiple expenses like fees, bills, a spike in tax, and more pop up after a budget is set and done. Modifying your financial plan every now and then is only obvious.

2. Budget is all about the nitty-gritty

Haven't you heard about the importance of jotting each piece of detail in a money plan?

Keeping tabs on the money that's rolling in and the outgoing expenditure certainly simplifies the task of budgeting. However, keeping track of a spreadsheet with countless items on the list to be marked off is not a cakewalk. Listing the details can put a restrain on your outrageous spending habits. But, better control of your finances is at the core of every budget plan.

The objective is to scale down all expenses and make room for more savings. An easy 50-30-20 money model can work wonders. Not sure what a 50-30-20 model stands for? Well, fifty refers to 50% of your earnings being used to foot all essential bills, taxes, and other necessities. 30% of the money can be put into miscellaneous expenses that are unplanned. 20% of your income is straight set out as savings. Regardless of the circumstances, curbing your savings is not an option. Cutting down on your miscellaneous expenditure can add to your savings.

3. Budgeting takes up all the time in the world

Do you fear preparing a budget thinking about the hours and days you need to invest? Making efficient financial plans is no hard labor. Monitoring your spending and keeping a close check on your account statements frequently is enough to help you kick-start a budget.

Get Out Of Debt On A Low Income

Sinking into outrageous debts is easier done than realized. Are you a bad spender or a greenhorn in matters of planning? If yes, bad debts are right around the corner. Struggling to swim out of debt? A meager and low-scale income certainly makes your way to recovery a hard nut to crack. But, kissing goodbye to big debts is possible. Don't worry about trading off your assets to square off the loans. You could clear the debts even when rolling in less money.

Wondering if there's a trick that works like magic? Maybe not tricks but proven strategies that pull you out of the pit. Paying off debt is much easy when you plan and rethink your expenditures. Let's put the limelight on a few realistic ways to stay clear of the burgeoning debts.

1. Monitor your income up and close

Of course, you have a clear idea about your take-home salary. But, can you dig deep and re-evaluate any other open income streams? Seldom do you realize that you might have an interest from an investment rolling in. Also, do not settle for a single source of earning when it pays peanuts. Get creative and engage in side hustles that could win you extra money.

2. Take a good look at your current financial standing

There's no way you can fix bad debts unless you acknowledge the hot waters you are in. To dwindle your debts, you must first list down all your debts. Jot down the details. For example, the interest piling, regular monthly payments, available credits, and so on so forth. Wondering why make an effort jotting down a list when everything is pretty clear in your head? A list hands you the big numbers to work upon in real-time. It is also a critical step in the making of a budget.

3. Cut down your discretionary expenses right away

Stop and think - are you throwing riches to bring your desires to fruition? How worthy does a fancy vacation sound when affording a stay-cation puts you in a pickle? Little do you realize that your discretionary income is affected. The objective is to increase your earnings and deplete stressful debts. Sticking to the old spending habits will only land you in the hot waters with debts shooting up. Stop spending a chunk of your income on subscriptions and streaming services. Hunt for cashback and make the best use of discount coupons when shopping essentials.

4. Get deep footed into investments

Sustaining on a meager income is challenging. Wondering how you could make room for investments? The right investments can win you big money. Does the thought of making good money help in easing your stress? Before you take the plunge and put in your money, study the various instruments and investment options thoroughly. Remember, a volatile market could sink your funds. Analyze what's safe and reaps you better profit - a retirement account or a brokerage one?

5. Switch to using cash and not credit

Not many speak about the pitfalls of using credits recklessly. If you are not too sure or responsible with your credit card, staying away from it can save you the horrors of spiking debts. Cashbacks and reward points can be very tempting. Don't fall for the trap. Use cash and toss out the credit cards. Your chances of slipping up and hurting your credit score are much less.

Strategies To Help Pay Off Credit Card Debt

Thoughtless swiping of credit cards for small and big purchases harms your finances. Are you looking into strategies that can win you relief from the burdening debts? Consolidation of the dues is an effective way out. There are various other smart strategies that dwindles credit card debts without much hassle.

1. Single out one debt, to begin with

Are you anxious scouting through the lengthy outstanding credit card statements? The dues certainly throw you in a pickle. As troubling as it may sound, targeting one card and squaring off the debt play a key role in the process. Puzzled which card to pick? Focus on choosing a card with the least amount of outstanding billed. Settling the smaller dues is less stressful.

If at all possible, save your funds and try and square off the outstanding all at once. When you pay off the less swanky dues first, you can shell out the money to foot the next credit card bill.

A smart tip:

Are multiple debts with similar dues a little too overwhelming for your muddled mind? Here's a hack that works:

Go through the statements with a fine-toothed comb. Figure and track down the card that bills you the highest interest. Paying off the debts on the selected card first is a good start. The sooner you settle the bills, the more you save from drowning your cash in paying down the richly interests and charges.

2. Think of resorting to debt consolidation

Debt consolidation is a promising option for those with good credit. Are you mostly in the sixes and sevens trying to settle multiple debts simultaneously? Consider consolidating all your dues into one. Paying down the credit card dues seems a lot hassle-free and less taxing on your mind. You can take out a personal loan to recoup the debts or avail the perks of fixed interest rates on debt consolidation loans.

Worried that a personal loan could charge you fat interests? Little are you familiar with the fact that the interests billed on personal loans are much less and cut-down than credit cards?

3. Do not be comfortable paying off the minimum balance on your credit card only

Squaring off the minimum balance charged on a credit card sounds a tad less burdening. What you often forget are the steep interests you are paying. Footing amounts more than the minimum amount accrued saves you big on interests.

Think about it - when you pay extra funds to recoup the debts, the bills on your overall outstanding dwindles. Certainly, there's a dip in the interest scored on the due amount.

4. Setting up a practicable budget

Not keeping tabs on your expenses is a big bummer. Preparing a financial plan that lists your income and spending matters big. Can you cut down the expenses of essential health care or education? No! The housing costs won't come down either. Set your priorities and identify areas where scaling down the expenses won't matter. When you free up your funds, mindlessly drained on non-essential things, you win more money to settle the credit card debts.

Tips To Slim Down Unnecessary Expenses

Are you a spendthrift? Do you go all out and spend riches without any thought? Little did you know that forking out money is a habit. A careless spender is mostly a waster. The odds of making hefty expenses are not unknown. Debt is the biggest downside of overspending. Staying on top of personal finance is not as easy as it sounds. The more you save, the better are you at recouping the big bad debts.

Curbing your spending out of the blue is hard-won. But, it is imperative to put a stop to your thoughtless spending pattern. Wondering how to stay clear from making big expenses? Let's share some tips.

1. Put your extra earnings into your savings

Are you employed in a side gig that pays you good money? Great! Instead of frittering out the cash on merriment, isn't it worth saving the big bucks? Don't you feel lucky to find a twenty-dollar bill tucked away in your pant pockets? Saving up the extra cash is a good idea. You can foster the nest egg and put your foot off the paddle instead of being dragged into massive debts.

2. Cut down on the coffee runs

There's nothing more blissful than having a spectacular barrister right around the corner. But, have you ever counted the dollars you are dishing out for a cup of Joe every day? Bearing the costs of coffee will stun you. Save spending the dollar on expensive barristers and make yourself a steaming cup of coffee at home. You can save as big as hundreds of dollars.

3. Say "No" to impulsive shopping

The downsides of impulsive shopping are way too many. Do you love forking out riches on exquisite shoes? The desire to add a new pair to your oversized collection stops you from spending the money recklessly. If you are cash-strapped, you rely on credit cards to wrap the purchase. Result? The debts keep piling.

If shopping fills your heart with joy, it might as well be worthy to set a cap limit every month. Label these expenses as miscellaneous. Regardless of the umpteen numbers of promos and discount coupons you are rewarded with, crossing the budget is a no-go.

4. Stop footing the bills for memberships and recreation

The recurring monthly bills are hard to keep tabs on. You end up spending a chunk of your earnings on subscriptions and memberships. Isn't it pointless to foot the bills for something that's insignificant? Warding out the unwanted expenses off your list casts a huge difference on your budget.

5. Do not drop into a grocery store without a list

Purchasing groceries sounds like a picnic, right? Well, without planning the list of items you need, you could go all out and pick up products that are of no use to you. Hopping into the store with a list keeps you focused and clear from being tempted to purchase products that appeal big to you.

6. Sell off the items from your closet

Do you love hoarding trendy pieces and exclusive clothes? Might as well start up a thrift store putting all your unused fine quality stuff for sale. You could earn money and clear the junk stacking up in your closet.

Saving the hard-earned dollars and trimming your spending can help you stay clear of debts.

To sum things up a bit, you really should think before shelling out your money on random things, especially when you have a high debt load. Stocking up on groceries makes sense but how worthy is it to stack up fancy shoes? Unnecessary spending can spiral out of control pretty quickly. Being watchful of your money and tapping your expenditures works wonders in accumulating bigger savings.

www.ingramcontent.com/pod-product-compliance
Lightning Source LLC
LaVergne TN
LVHW080559160826
845677LV00010B/1910
9798355309541